PENGUIN BOOKS
THE MAD, MAD WORLD OF CRICKET

**Sudhir Dar** was born in 1932 at Allahabad. He took a master's degree in geography and worked as a broadcaster with All India Radio and later with Air-India doing sales promotion. He came to cartooning in 1960, creating a witty, wordless cartoon series for the *Statesman* (Delhi and Calcutta). In 1967 he joined the *Hindustan Times* where he spent over two decades drawing political cartoons and a daily pocket cartoon called 'This Is It!'. He worked with the *Pioneer* in Delhi for the next seven years, before moving to the *Delhi Times*, a daily supplement of the *Times of India*. Dar's cartoons have also appeared in the *New York Times*, the *Washington Post* and *Saturday Review*. *Mad* magazine once called him a 'Tasty Indian Nut'.

The recipient of numerous national and international awards, Dar's poster calendar for Air-India won awards at the 1980 International CLIO awards in the USA. He also represented India at the first International Cartoonists' Conference in London in 1970. Many of his originals are now part of private collections including those of Queen Elizabeth II, Lord Richard Attenborough, Henry Kissinger and the late Yehudi Menuhin.

Sudhir Dar is married and has two daughters. He lives in Delhi.

# The Mad, Mad World of Cricket

Sudhir Dar

**PENGUIN BOOKS**

An imprint of Penguin Random House

PENGUIN BOOKS

USA | Canada | UK | Ireland | Australia
New Zealand | India | South Africa | China | Singapore

Penguin Books is part of the Penguin Random House group
of companies whose addresses can be found at global.
penguinrandomhouse.com

Published by Penguin Random House India Pvt. Ltd
4th Floor, Capital Tower 1, MG Road,
Gurugram 122 002, Haryana, India

First published by Penguin Books India 2007

Copyright © Sudhir Dar 2007

All rights reserved

10 9 8 7 6 5 4

ISBN 9780143101840

Printed at Manipal Technologies Limited, India

www.penguin.co.in

MIX
Paper | Supporting
responsible forestry
FSC® C043100

This is a legitimate digitally printed version of the book and therefore might not
have certain extra finishing on the cover.

To the Men in Blue...
with all Good Wishes

## Publisher's Note

For several decades now, Sudhir Dar has regaled readers with his inimitable creations. This volume contains some of his best cricket cartoons, including some new and topical additions. Published in time for the 2007 cricket World Cup, this collection will delight every fan who loves the magic and madness of cricket.

"INDIA VS. PAKISTAN!"

"I GET ONE TOO... WHEN INDIA PLAYS PAKISTAN!"

"DON'T YOU DARE!! TAKE THAT RIGHT BACK WHERE IT BELONGS!!"

"DID YOU HEAR THE ONE ABOUT SHANE WARNE AND MALLIKA SHERAWAT..?!"

"MUST BE THE NEW SPINNER!"

"BEFORE A TEST WE NEED A PEP **TALK**...NOT A PEP **PILL!**"

"IS RICKY PONTING STILL BOWLING..?!"

"YOUR ATTENTION, PLEASE! DUE TO TECHNICAL REASONS, THERE'LL BE A DELAY IN AIR-INDIA FLIGHT NO.."

10

13

14

"GUYS, PLEASE, I'M NOT SUPPOSED TO **LIFT WEIGHTS** – I'VE HAD A SLIPPED DISC!!"

"COME ON, RELAX, RELAX — YOU'VE FACED SHOAIB AKHTAR BEFORE!"

17

"WOW, WHAT A SIX!"

"NOT EASY SOMETIMES... BEING MARRIED TO AN EX-CRICKETER!"

21

22

"GENTLEMEN...TONIGHT, OUR CHEF HAS PREPARED SOMETHING VERY SPECIAL, JUST FOR YOU... **DUCK!**"

27

28

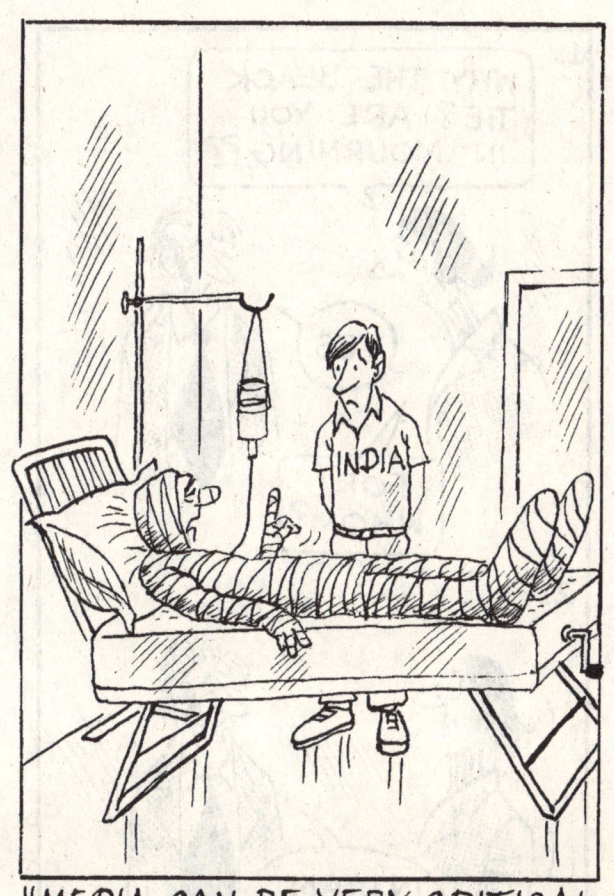

"MEDIA CAN BE VERY CRITICAL BUT FANS CAN BE MUCH WORSE—HIGHLY INJURIOUS TO HEALTH !!"

33

36

"NEVER MIND, HAVE SOME TEA... 'THE CUP THAT CHEERS'!"

"CONGRATULATIONS, YOUR WIFE
JUST HIT A 'FOUR' - SHE'S HAD
QUADRUPLETS !!"

"OH, PLEASE..DON'T..DON'T..MY
HAIR IS A MESS !"

"OH, OH... THERE GOES **OUR** 'MASTER BLASTER'!!"

"BED TEA FOR **DHONI!** CAN I TAKE IT?!"

41

"OK, THAT'S ENOUGH...NOW LET'S GET BACK TO THE GAME!"

"MY GOD, WHAT A BOUNCY PITCH...!"

"OYE, BALLE-BALLE!!"

"INDIA WON!"

51

"MAY THE BETTER SIDE **LOSE!**"

"BHAI SAHAB, HAVE A LADDOO. AUSTRALIA'S **OUT**!"

"THERE'S ONLY ONE WAY WE CAN SAVE FACE NOW...PLAY FIJI OR TONGA!"

55

"NEVER SEEN SUCH A BIASED UMPIRE..!"

"WHY GO TO SHARJAH IF ALL THEY CAN DO IS 'HARJAH'.?!"

"WHAT A FIELDER — NEVER MISSES A CATCH!"

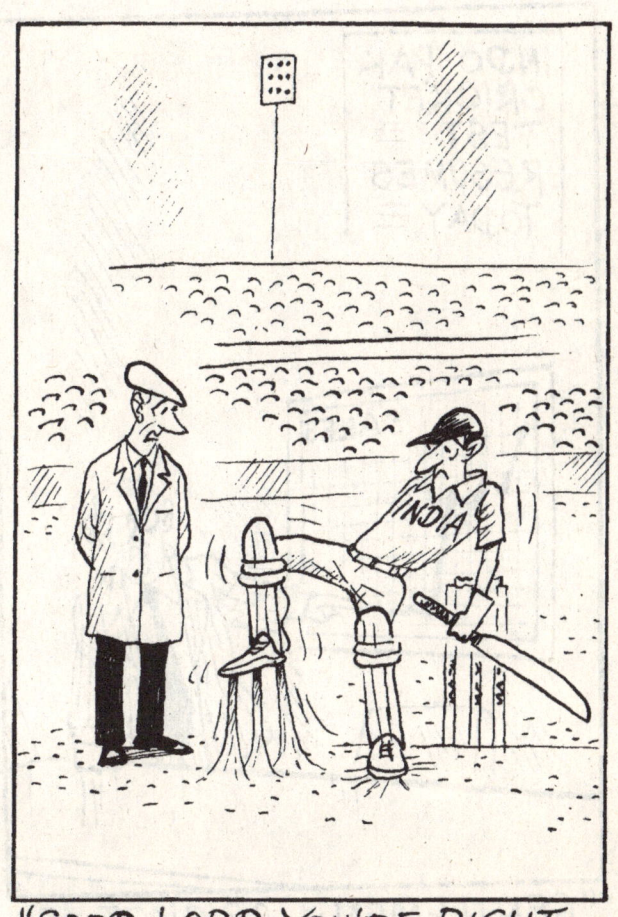

"GOOD LORD, YOU'RE RIGHT—
THIS **IS** A STICKY WICKET!"

"GENTLEMEN... CRICKET IS DESTROYING THIS COMPANY!"

63

"CHEERS!!"

TEA-BREAK!

"WHEN IT COMES TO TEA-BREAKS,
YOU CAN'T BEAT THE OLD MASTERS
OF THE GAME..!"

"DRINKS!!"

68

"OK, OK, I'M SORRY I WROTE THAT, I APOLOGISE — YOU **ARE** IN FORM!!"

"DOWN WITH HINDI !!"

"BECAUSE HE HATES SERIALS AND I HATE CRICKET!"

"WAKE ME WHEN IRFAN PATHAN COMES..!"

"SHOULDN'T THE GAME BE ABANDONED FOR THE DAY...!"

"IN THIS COUNTRY IT'S NOT A GAME, IT'S AN **OBSESSION..!**"

"IT'S A FOUR!"

"WATCH OUT, SUNNY...PLENTY OF **'BODYLINE'** HERE!"

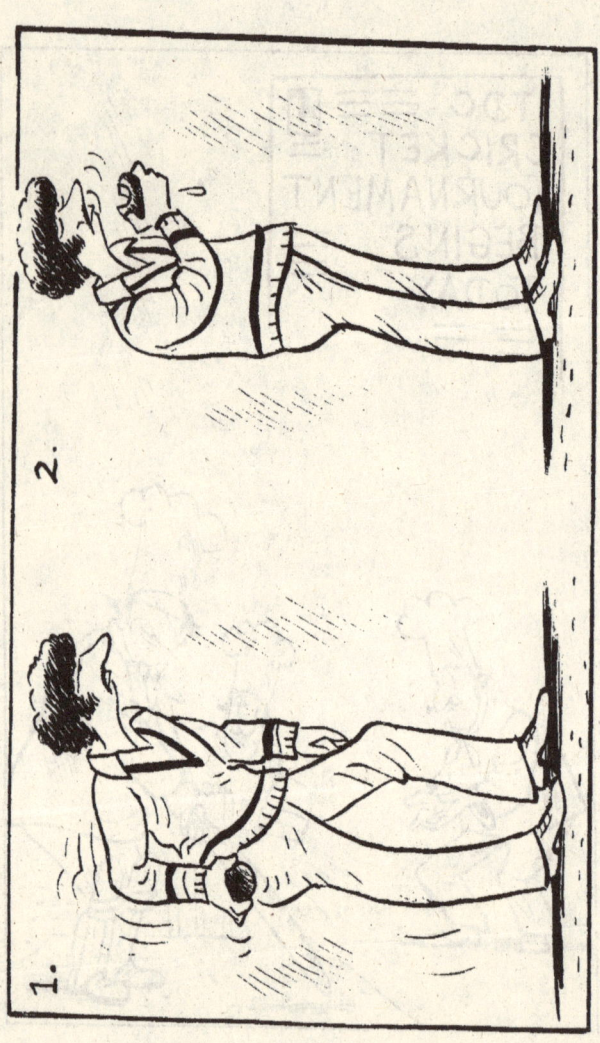

80

"COME ON, GUYS, WAKE UP, IT'S TIME
TO PRACTICE! WE DIDN'T COME TO GOA
JUST TO GET **ACCLIMATISED**!"

"YA. YA IN HALF-AN-HOUR...!"

"**FIRST** YOU CHANGE THE FUSED BULB IN THE KITCHEN..!"

"WORLD CUP!"